CONTENTS

INTRODUCTION

Hey there, friend! Are you looking to take your life to the next level? Are you ready to invest in yourself and achieve personal growth? Well, you've come to the right place because in this book, we're going to dive deep into the world of personal development.

We're going to cover the 7 pillars of personal development, which are essential for achieving a fulfilling and successful life. These pillars include taking care of our mind, body, soul, finances, career, family, and social life. By focusing on these areas, we can create a solid foundation for personal growth.

But that's not all. We're also going to talk about habits - the good, the bad, and the ugly. We'll discuss how to form new habits, how to break bad ones, and how to make lasting changes in our lives.

And let's not forget about goal setting. I've developed my own SMASHIT framework for setting and achieving goals, which we'll dive into in-depth. By following this framework, you'll be able to set goals that are Specific, Measurable, Achievable, Relevant, Time-bound, Holistic, Inspirational, and Tailored to you.

But personal development isn't just about these areas. We'll also explore other important topics such as time management, productivity, stress management, and communication. By focusing on all these areas, we can create a well-rounded approach to personal growth and development.

So, whether you're just starting your personal development journey or you're a seasoned pro, this book is for you. I'll provide practical tips, tools, and strategies that you can implement in your life right away. So, let's get started on this journey together and create the life you've always dreamed of.

CHAPTER 1: THE 7 PILLARS OF PERSONAL DEVELOPMENT

Welcome to the 7 pillars of personal development! These seven areas are the foundation for a fulfilling and successful life, and it's important to focus on each one to achieve overall personal growth.

The mind pillar focuses on mental health, including things like mindfulness, learning new skills, and managing stress and anxiety. The body pillar is all about physical health, including exercise, nutrition, and self-care.

The soul pillar is centred around spiritual and emotional well-being, which can include meditation, gratitude practices, and pursuing hobbies or passions that bring us joy. The finances pillar is all about managing money, including budgeting, investing, and building wealth.

The career pillar focuses on professional development and achieving success in our chosen career paths, including setting goals and developing new skills. The family pillar emphasises the importance of healthy and supportive relationships with loved ones, including communication, quality time, and boundary-setting.

And finally, the social life pillar is all about building and maintaining positive relationships with friends and community, including finding ways to give back and be involved in our communities.

By focusing on each of these pillars and working to improve in each area, we can achieve a more balanced and fulfilling life. So, let's dive into each of these pillars and explore how we can work to improve our personal development in each area.

Mind

Let me tell you why having a positive mindset is crucial for personal development. A positive mindset helps you bounce back from setbacks and challenges. Instead of dwelling on negative thoughts and feelings, a positive mindset helps you focus on solutions and opportunities. A positive mindset can also reduce stress and anxiety, leading to improved mental health. It can help you see the positive aspects of your life and appreciate what you have. When you have a positive outlook, you are more likely to think outside the box and come up with new ideas. Furthermore, a positive mindset can boost your self-esteem and confidence. When you believe in yourself and your abilities, you are more likely to take risks and pursue your goals. A positive mindset can also improve your relationships with others. When you approach others with positivity and optimism, you are more likely to build strong, healthy relationships based on trust and respect.

On the other hand, a fixed mindset can lead to feelings of helplessness, a fear of failure, and a reluctance to take on challenges or try new things. People with a growth mindset embrace challenges, persist through obstacles, and see effort as a necessary part of success. By consciously adopting a growth mindset, people can cultivate a willingness to learn and grow, and ultimately achieve their goals.

Developing a growth mindset involves adopting a belief that one's abilities and intelligence can be developed and improved over time through hard work, dedication, and perseverance. You can start by embracing challenges instead of avoiding them. Focus on the process of learning and the effort you put in instead of just the outcome. Learn from your failures, keep learning, practice self-reflection, and surround yourself with positive influences. With practice, you can learn to embrace challenges, learn from failures, and continue to grow and develop throughout your life.

Your self-talk can significantly impact your self-esteem, mood, and overall well-being. Positive self-talk involves encouraging, motivating, and supportive thoughts, while negative self-talk involves self-criticism, self-doubt, and negative thoughts. By practicing positive self-talk, you can improve your self-esteem, boost your confidence, and enhance your ability to cope with challenges.

To work on your own self-talk, start by noticing your self-talk throughout the day. Evaluate your self-talk to determine if it is helpful or harmful. Challenge negative self-talk by questioning its validity, and replace it with positive self-talk. By working on your self-talk, you can improve your mental well-being and achieve your goals. Remember, developing a positive mindset and a growth mindset is a process that takes time and effort, but the rewards are worth it.

Body

I couldn't agree more with the statement that good health is one of the most important factors in personal development. It's amazing how much of an impact our physical and mental well-being can have on our lives.

Let's start with physical health. Our bodies are amazing machines that require regular maintenance to function at their best. Exercise and a healthy diet are two of the most important things we can do to keep our bodies in tip-top shape. Exercise not only helps to keep us physically fit but also releases endorphins, which can improve our mood and reduce stress. And eating a balanced diet that includes plenty of fruits, vegetables, whole grains, and lean protein can help prevent chronic diseases like heart disease and diabetes.

Now let's talk about mental health. Our minds need care too! Managing stress, practicing mindfulness, and seeking support from loved ones or mental health professionals are all great ways to take care of our mental health. When we take care of our mental health, we can build resilience, cope with stress, and cultivate positive relationships.

The benefits of good health go beyond just physical and mental well-being. When we feel healthy and energised, we're more likely to have the confidence to pursue our goals and try new things. We're also more likely to form positive relationships with others and enjoy more of life's experiences.

So how can we improve our health? There are plenty of ways! Regular exercise, a healthy diet, getting enough sleep, managing stress, staying hydrated, avoiding smoking and excessive alcohol consumption, practicing good hygiene, and getting regular check-ups with our healthcare providers are all important steps we can take to improve our health.

Remember, good health isn't something that can be achieved overnight. It's a journey, and small changes in our daily habits can make a big difference over time. So let's take care of ourselves, both physically and mentally, and enjoy all the benefits that good health has to offer!

Soul

Spirituality can mean different things to different people, and there is no one "right" way to engage in spiritual practices. Some individuals may find that meditation or prayer is helpful for them, while others may find that spending time in nature or engaging in creative pursuits helps them connect with their spirituality. Whatever form spirituality takes for an individual, the important thing is that it provides them with a sense of purpose, meaning, and connection to something greater than themselves.

One of the benefits of spirituality is increased self-awareness. By engaging in practices that encourage introspection and reflection, individuals can develop a deeper understanding of themselves and their emotions. This increased self-awareness can help individuals identify and work through personal issues, leading to personal growth and development. When individuals understand their own values and beliefs, they can make more informed decisions about their lives, leading to a more fulfilling life.

Spirituality can also have a positive impact on mental and emotional health. Studies have shown that engaging in spiritual practices such as meditation or prayer can reduce symptoms of anxiety, depression, and stress. Spiritual practices can help individuals develop coping mechanisms to manage negative emotions and improve their overall well-being.

Another benefit of spirituality is a greater sense of purpose and meaning. Spirituality provides individuals with a sense of purpose and meaning beyond material possessions and external achievements. This can lead to a greater sense of fulfilment and satisfaction in life. When individuals have a clear sense of purpose, they are motivated to pursue their goals and aspirations, leading to a more purposeful life.

Spirituality can also enhance relationships. By promoting empathy, compassion, and understanding, spiritual practices can help individuals develop deeper and more meaningful relationships with others. When individuals feel connected to others on a deeper level, they are more likely to communicate effectively, resolve conflicts peacefully, and build stronger relationships.

Spirituality can also provide individuals with a greater sense of resilience in the face of challenges and adversity. By providing individuals with a sense of hope and comfort during difficult times, spiritual practices can help individuals bounce back from setbacks and continue to grow and develop.

To come to the point, spirituality can be a powerful

tool for personal development, helping individuals to become more self-aware, mentally and emotionally healthy, purposeful, compassionate, and resilient. Whatever form spirituality takes for an individual, the important thing is that it provides them with a sense of purpose, meaning, and connection to something greater than themselves.

Finance

I'm excited to share with you why finance is essential for personal development. Finance plays a crucial role in providing the necessary resources to achieve our goals and objectives, allowing us to pursue our passions and interests without financial constraints. Financial stability and security are the building blocks of a fulfilling life. Let's explore some reasons why finance is crucial for personal development.

Firstly, adequate finances are required to meet the basic needs of food, clothing, and shelter. Without financial security, individuals may struggle to meet their daily expenses, which can have a significant impact on their quality of life. Secondly, financial stability is necessary to achieve personal goals, such as purchasing a home, starting a business, or pursuing higher education. Financial resources provide individuals with the means to invest in themselves and achieve their objectives.

Thirdly, having a sound understanding of personal finance helps individuals to manage risks and prepare for unexpected expenses. Emergency funds and insurance policies can protect individuals from financial hardships caused by unforeseen events such as illness, accidents, or job loss. Fourthly, financial stress can have a significant impact on an individual's mental and physical health. Financial stability provides peace of mind and reduces stress levels, allowing individuals to focus on their personal growth and development.

Lastly, investing and saving money can help individuals build long-term wealth, providing financial security and stability for the future. This financial security allows individuals to take risks, pursue opportunities, and continue to grow and develop over time.

To live a financially healthy and stable life, it's important to follow some key financial principles. Spend less than you earn, create a budget, save for emergencies, invest for the long-term, pay off debt, maximise your retirement savings, live within your means, and keep track of your credit score. By following these principles, you can build a strong foundation for your financial future and achieve your long-term goals.

Getting started on your financial journey may seem overwhelming, but it doesn't have to be. Assess your current financial situation, set financial goals, create a budget, track your spending, pay off high-interest debt, start saving for emergencies, start investing, and monitor your progress. Remember, the most important thing is to get started. Even small steps towards financial health can make a big difference in the long run.

There are many resources available to help you achieve your financial goals. Financial advisors are professionals who can help you with financial planning, investments, retirement planning, and other aspects of personal finance. Non-profit credit counselling agencies can help you manage your debts and create a budget. Online resources such as budgeting apps, financial blogs, and podcasts can provide you with tips and advice on personal finance.

Finance is essential for personal development. Financial stability and security provide individuals with the necessary resources to achieve their goals and objectives, allowing them to lead a fulfilling life. By following key financial principles and getting started on your financial journey, you can build a strong foundation for your financial future and achieve your long-term goals.

Career

I want to tell you about why reflecting on your career journey is so important. Whether you're just starting out or you've been working for years, taking time to reflect on your career can provide numerous benefits.

Firstly, reflection helps you gain self-awareness about your career journey, including your strengths, weaknesses, and values. By understanding your strengths and weaknesses, you can make more informed career decisions that align with your goals and values.

Secondly, reflection allows you to identify areas for growth and development. By reflecting on your career journey, you can identify what has worked well for you in the past, what hasn't worked, and what you can do differently moving forward. This knowledge can help you grow and develop in your career.

Thirdly, reflection allows you to appreciate the progress you have made in your career journey. This can help you feel more grateful and satisfied with your career, which can lead to increased motivation and productivity.

Fourthly, reflection can help you make more informed career decisions. By reflecting on your past experiences and lessons learned, you can make better decisions about your future career goals and actions.

Finally, reflection can help build confidence in your career journey. By reflecting on your past successes and challenges, you can build confidence in your abilities and make more informed decisions about your future career path.

In addition to reflecting on your own career journey, having a career mentor can be a valuable resource. A career mentor can provide guidance, support, and advice based on their own experiences and expertise. They can help with job search strategies, networking, career development, professional growth, and overcoming challenges in the workplace.

Building a network is also essential for advancing your career and achieving your goals. This can be done through attending networking events, joining professional organisations, utilising social media, attending conferences and trade shows, volunteering, and following up with new connections.

Stepping outside of your comfort zone can also lead to new experiences, skills, and opportunities. It can help you learn and grow, gain new perspectives, and build confidence in yourself and your abilities. However, it's important to find a balance between pushing yourself outside of your comfort zone and taking care of your mental health and well-being.

Lastly, making a change in your career can be a scary decision, but with careful consideration and planning, it can lead to a successful transition. Reflect on your current situation, identify your strengths and weaknesses, research your desired career path, and take actionable steps towards your goals.

Remember, reflecting on your career journey is an ongoing process. It's important to take time to evaluate your career path, set goals and make adjustments as needed to ensure that you are constantly growing and developing in your chosen profession. Regularly assessing your skills, strengths, and weaknesses, as well as considering new opportunities and challenges, can help you stay on track and achieve the career success and fulfilment you desire. Don't be afraid to seek guidance and support from mentors, colleagues, and other resources as you navigate your career journey. Your career is a journey, not a destination, and with thoughtful reflection and intentional action, you can continue to progress and thrive in your chosen field.

Family

From birth, family members are the first socialisation agents that teach us about social norms, values, beliefs, and expectations.

Moreover, they are the ones who teach us essential skills like communication, problem-solving, and relationships, which are crucial for personal growth.

The family environment, including parenting styles, family structure, and relationships between family members, has a profound impact on an individual's personal development. Children who grow up in a supportive and nurturing family environment are more likely to develop positive self-esteem, social skills, and emotional intelligence. In contrast, children who grow up in an environment characterised by neglect, abuse, or conflict may struggle with issues such as low self-esteem, depression, anxiety, and relationship problems.

Family members also serve as role models for personal development by demonstrating positive behaviours and attitudes. Parents who model empathy, kindness, and self-control can positively influence their children's personal development. As you can see, having a close family can have many benefits for personal development, including emotional support, a sense of belonging, role models, communication skills, and shared values.

To develop a strong family bond, it takes effort and commitment from all family members. Some tips for building a strong family bond include communication, shared activities, support, respect, and traditions. By prioritising these elements, you can build a strong and lasting family bond.

Of course, challenges within the family are a natural part of life, and every family goes through tough times. Strategies for overcoming these challenges include communication, empathy, compromise, seeking outside help, and forgiveness. Remember, overcoming challenges within the family takes time and effort, but with these strategies, you can work towards a stronger and healthier family dynamic.

Family plays a significant role in personal development, and having a close family can have a positive impact on one's overall well-being and success in life. Family members provide emotional support, encouragement, and guidance, which can help individuals navigate challenges and achieve their goals. Moreover, a close family can foster a sense of belonging and connectedness, which is crucial for building strong social relationships and developing a healthy self-esteem. Overall, the family serves as a fundamental unit of society and plays a crucial role in shaping individuals' character, values, and identity.

Social

The importance of socialising in personal development is something that I believe is often overlooked, but has numerous benefits for our growth and well-being.

Firstly, socialising helps us develop social skills. When we interact with others, we learn valuable skills such as communication, empathy, active listening, conflict resolution, and cooperation. These skills are not only important for personal relationships, but they can also be beneficial in the workplace.

Another benefit of socialising is that it expands our horizons. Meeting and interacting with people from different backgrounds and with different perspectives can expose us to new ideas and experiences. This can help us grow and develop as individuals.

Socialising can also boost our confidence and self-esteem. When we connect with others and receive positive feedback, we can feel more secure in ourselves and our abilities.

Perhaps one of the most important benefits of socialising is its positive impact on our mental health. Being part of a social network provides emotional support and can reduce stress, anxiety, and depression. In fact, research has shown that social support is a key factor in mental health and overall well-being.

Networking is another benefit of socialising. By meeting new people, we can build professional networks and potentially connect with job opportunities, mentors, and other professional resources.

Now, let's talk about finding the right people to socialise with. This is important for several reasons. Firstly, socialising with people who share similar interests can be more enjoyable and fulfilling. It can also be helpful to be around positive, supportive, and uplifting people, as they can boost our mood and outlook on life. On the other hand, being around negative, unsupportive, or toxic people can have the opposite effect.

Socialising with people who challenge us and encourage personal growth can also be highly beneficial. They can offer new perspectives, push us to take risks, and provide constructive feedback. Spending time with people who share similar values can also help us feel more understood and validated.

To find the right social circle, it's important to consider our own values, interests, and goals, and seek out individuals who align with these aspects of our personality. This can be achieved by joining clubs or groups centred around our hobbies, attending networking events or conferences related to our career, or simply reaching out to acquaintances who share common interests. It's also important to keep an open mind and be willing to step outside of our comfort zone to meet new people and broaden our perspective. Ultimately, building a strong and supportive social network can have a positive impact on our overall well-being and personal growth.

CHAPTER 2: THE POWER OF PERSONAL DEVELOPMENT

Personal development is the process of improving oneself through intentional efforts and activities. It involves setting goals, developing skills, and improving one's mindset and attitude towards life. I passionately believe in the power of personal development, as it has transformed my life in countless ways.

One of the greatest benefits of personal development is increased self-awareness. Through self-reflection, goal-setting, and mindfulness practices, I have gained a deeper understanding of my values, beliefs, and priorities. This self-awareness has helped me make better decisions that align with my goals and values, and has enabled me to recognise my own biases and blind spots.

Another powerful aspect of personal development is the acquisition of new skills and knowledge. Whether it's learning a new language, developing a skill for work, or improving my communication skills, I have found that continuous learning and growth has opened up countless opportunities for me. By investing in myself through education and training, I have been able to advance in my career and personal life.

Perhaps the most impactful benefit of personal development is the improvement in one's mindset and attitude. By practicing positive self-talk, gratitude, and mindfulness, I have been able to shift my mindset from one of self-doubt and negativity to one of optimism and abundance. This shift has enabled me to overcome challenges and setbacks with resilience and perseverance, and has allowed me to approach life with a greater sense of purpose and meaning.

Personal development is not a one-time event, but rather a lifelong journey. It requires consistent effort and dedication to improve oneself and reach one's full potential. While it can be challenging at times, the rewards are immeasurable. Through personal development, I have become a better version of myself and have been able to make a positive impact on those around me.

Personal development is a powerful tool for growth and transformation. It enables us to become more self-aware, acquire new skills and knowledge, and improve our mindset and attitude towards life. By investing in ourselves and committing to personal development, we can unlock our full potential and live a fulfilling and meaningful life.

Self-Awareness

Self-awareness is a vital component of personal growth and development as it involves a deep understanding of oneself. Being self-aware means having the ability to recognise and understand our thoughts, emotions, behaviours, and personality traits, and how they impact our daily interactions with the people around us.

Through self-awareness, we are able to gain insights into our strengths, weaknesses, and areas for improvement. This allows us to identify patterns and behaviours that may be holding us back from achieving our goals and making positive changes to overcome them. By recognising our strengths, we can leverage them to achieve success, while identifying our weaknesses can help us develop strategies to improve.

Moreover, self-awareness helps us make more informed decisions as it provides us with a better understanding of our needs, values, and beliefs. We become better equipped to evaluate situations and make choices that align with our goals and values, which in turn, can lead to greater fulfilment and happiness.

In addition, self-awareness plays a crucial role in improving our relationships with others. By understanding our emotions and how they impact our interactions with others, we can become more empathetic, compassionate, and understanding. We also become more aware of how our actions and words affect others, which can lead to more positive and authentic connections.

Self-awareness can be defined as the ability to recognise and understand one's own thoughts, feelings, and behaviours, and how they impact ourselves and others. It can be divided into two states: internal self-awareness and external self-awareness.

Internal self-awareness involves understanding our own emotions, values, beliefs, and thought patterns. It means being able to recognise our own strengths and weaknesses and being honest with ourselves about our limitations. When we are internally self-aware, we can identify what motivates us, what our goals are, and what drives our behaviour. This helps us to make more informed decisions and take actions that are in line with our values and priorities.

External self-awareness, on the other hand, involves understanding how our actions, behaviours, and emotions impact others. This requires us to be attuned to the emotions and needs of those around us, and to be able to empathise with them. When we are externally self-aware, we are able to recognise how our behaviour affects others, and we can adjust our actions accordingly. This helps us to build stronger relationships with others, as we are better able to understand and meet their needs.

Both internal and external self-awareness are important for personal growth and development. By developing our internal self-awareness, we can identify areas for growth, recognise our own biases and limitations, and work to improve our own behaviour. By developing our external self-awareness, we can build stronger relationships with others, communicate more effectively, and create a more positive impact on the world around us. Ultimately, self-awareness allows us to become more authentic, empathetic, and effective individuals, leading to a more fulfilling and satisfying life.

As someone who has experienced the benefits of self-awareness first-hand, I can say that it's a crucial aspect of becoming the best version of yourself.

First and foremost, self-awareness helps individuals make better decisions. When you have a clear understanding of your own values, beliefs, and priorities, you can make more informed decisions that align with your goals and values. Being self-aware also helps you recognise your own biases, enabling you to make more objective decisions.

In addition, self-awareness helps individuals communicate more effectively. Understanding how your own behaviour and emotions affect others is key to building strong relationships. By being aware of your own communication style, you can tailor your approach to different situations and people, resulting in better outcomes.

Self-awareness also leads to increased emotional intelligence. Emotional intelligence involves the ability to recognise and manage one's own emotions, as well as the emotions of others. When you are aware of your own emotional state, you can better manage your reactions and respond in a more constructive manner. This skill can be applied in various aspects of life, such as in personal relationships and in the workplace.

Another benefit of self-awareness is personal growth. By recognising your own strengths and weaknesses, you can work on areas where you need improvement. This self-reflection and willingness to learn and grow can lead to significant personal development.

Finally, self-awareness can lead to better conflict resolution. When you are aware of your own role in conflicts, you can work towards resolving them in a constructive manner. This involves recognising the emotions and perspectives of others and being willing to communicate and compromise.

Have you ever heard of the self-awareness gap? It's actually quite interesting! The self-awareness gap is the difference between how we perceive ourselves and how others perceive us. This can happen because we tend to have biases and blind spots that make it difficult to see ourselves accurately.

The self-awareness gap can have negative consequences for us, especially in our relationships and professional settings. For instance, if we overestimate our abilities and fail to recognise our weaknesses, we may struggle to grow or advance in our careers. Similarly, if we don't understand how our behaviour affects others, we may have a hard time building and maintaining strong relationships.

But don't worry! There are ways to close the self-awareness gap. By engaging in practices such as self-reflection, seeking feedback from others, and assessing our own behaviour and thought patterns, we can develop a more accurate understanding of ourselves. This, in turn, can lead to improved relationships, better decision-making, and greater success in various aspects of our lives.

If you're a self-aware person, you may recognise some of the following characteristics in yourself:

1. You're able to recognise your own emotions and describe them accurately.

2. You're aware of your strengths and weaknesses, and actively work to improve yourself.

3. You have a clear understanding of your values, beliefs, and priorities.

4. You can recognise your own biases and try to remain objective in your decision-making.

5. You're open to feedback and actively seek it out to improve yourself.

6. You can regulate your own emotions and behaviour, even in challenging situations.

7. You're able to recognise how your behaviour impacts others and adjust accordingly.

8. You can communicate effectively and empathise with others.

9. You can adapt to change and are open to new experiences.

If you exhibit these characteristics, you're likely a highly self-aware person. However, self-awareness is a journey, and even self-aware individuals may struggle with certain aspects of their personality or behaviour. The important thing is to continue engaging in self-reflection and seeking feedback from others to improve and grow.

Are you looking to become more self-aware? Great news! I've got some strategies that can help you on your journey. By practicing these strategies, you can gain a deeper understanding of your thoughts, emotions, and behaviours, and how they impact yourself and others. Here are some strategies that can help you become more self-aware:

1. Practice mindfulness: Mindfulness is all about paying attention to the present moment without judgment. By being present and aware, you can gain insight into your thoughts, emotions, and physical sensations, which can increase your self-awareness.

2. Engage in self-reflection: Take time regularly to reflect on your thoughts, emotions, and behaviour. You can do this through journaling, meditation, or simply taking time to think about your day. By doing so, you can develop a deeper understanding of yourself and your reactions to different situations.

3. Seek feedback from others: Asking friends, family members, or colleagues for honest feedback on your

behaviour and how you are perceived by others can be a great way to gain perspective and identify areas where you may need to work on your self-awareness.

4. Take personality assessments: There are various personality assessments available that can help you gain insight into your personality traits, values, and strengths and weaknesses. This can help you identify areas for personal growth and development.

5. Practice active listening: By paying close attention to what others are saying and empathising with their perspective, you can become more aware of your own communication style and how it impacts others. This can also help you develop stronger relationships with those around you.

6. Be open to learning: Being willing to learn from new experiences and trying new things can help you gain a better understanding of yourself and your values. This can also help you identify areas for personal growth and development.

7. Seek the help of a therapist or coach: A trained professional can help you identify areas where you may lack self-awareness and provide guidance on how to improve. This can be particularly helpful if you are struggling to identify your blind spots or areas where you may be lacking in self-awareness.

Remember, becoming more self-aware takes time and effort. But by practicing these strategies, you can gain a deeper understanding of yourself and your impact on others, leading to personal growth and stronger relationships. So, give these strategies a try and see how they can help you on your journey towards greater self-awareness.

Improved Relationships

Personal development is a powerful tool that can positively impact every aspect of your life, including your personal and professional relationships. When you work on your personal growth, you develop skills and qualities that help you interact with others in more meaningful and effective ways.

One of the most significant ways personal development can improve your relationships is by improving your communication skills. When you invest time and energy in understanding yourself better, you become more aware of your communication style and can adjust it to better meet the needs of those around you. You learn to express your thoughts and feelings clearly, listen attentively, and respond thoughtfully, leading to better communication with your loved ones and colleagues.

In addition to communication skills, personal development can also help you develop greater empathy. Empathy is the ability to understand and share the feelings of others. As you become more self-aware and work on understanding your own emotions, you also become better able to understand the emotions of others. This deeper level of understanding can help you connect with others on a more personal level and build stronger relationships.

Personal development can also equip you with better conflict resolution skills. As you learn more about yourself and your own tendencies, you become better equipped to handle conflicts with others. You approach conflicts with a problem-solving mindset and seek solutions that benefit everyone involved, leading to more harmonious relationships.

Finally, personal development can help you develop greater emotional intelligence. Emotional intelligence is the ability to recognise and regulate your own emotions, as well as understand and respond to the emotions of others. When you have greater emotional intelligence, you are better able to manage your own emotions, connect with others on a deeper level, and navigate challenging situations with greater ease.

There we have it. Personal development can make you a better communicator, a more empathetic person, and a more emotionally intelligent individual, all of which can greatly benefit your personal and professional relationships. By investing in your personal growth, you invest in the quality of your relationships and ultimately, your overall well-being.

Career

As I've progressed in my career, I've come to appreciate the importance of personal development. In addition to the intrinsic rewards of learning and growth, personal development can have a significant impact on one's career prospects. Let's look at some ways in which it can help.

First, personal development can improve your skills and knowledge, making you more valuable to your current employer and more competitive in the job market. By acquiring new technical or soft skills, you become better equipped to tackle new challenges and take on more responsibilities. This can lead to greater job satisfaction and potentially even promotions or higher salaries.

Second, personal development can increase your self-awareness. When you understand your own strengths and weaknesses, you can better leverage your strengths and work on improving your weaknesses. This can help you build better relationships with colleagues, clients, and managers and ultimately enhance your career prospects. Additionally, self-awareness can help you navigate challenging situations and conflicts more effectively, leading to better outcomes and less stress.

Third, personal development can help you develop greater adaptability. In today's rapidly changing work environment, the ability to adjust to new situations and challenges is becoming increasingly important. As you develop greater adaptability, you become more resilient and better equipped to handle unexpected changes in your career. This can make you a more attractive candidate for new roles and opportunities.

Finally, personal development can help you enhance your leadership skills. Even if you are not currently in a leadership role, developing communication, problem-solving, and decision-making skills can make you a more capable and effective leader. This can lead to greater career opportunities and advancement.

Overall, personal development is a powerful tool for enhancing your career prospects. By acquiring new skills and knowledge, increasing self-awareness, developing adaptability, and enhancing leadership skills, you can position yourself for greater success and fulfilment in your career.

Personal development can enhance your career prospects is by improving your skills and knowledge. By pursuing personal development, you can acquire new technical or soft skills that are relevant to your career. For example, if you work in a tech industry, you may choose to learn a new programming language or development tool that is in demand. Alternatively, you may decide to work on your communication or leadership skills, which are important for most careers. As you acquire new skills and knowledge, you become more valuable to your current employer and more competitive in the job market.

Another way that personal development can enhance your career prospects is by increasing your self-awareness. When you work on personal development, you are encouraged to reflect on your strengths, weaknesses, and values. By becoming more self-aware, you can leverage your strengths and work on improving your weaknesses. This can help you build better relationships with colleagues, clients, and managers, and ultimately enhance your career prospects.

Personal development can also help you develop greater adaptability, which is increasingly important in today's rapidly changing work environment. As you develop greater adaptability, you become more resilient and better equipped to handle unexpected changes in your career. For example, you may be better able to adapt to changes in technology or changes in your industry.

Finally, personal development can enhance your career prospects by helping you develop leadership skills, even if you are not currently in a leadership role. As you develop your communication, problem-solving, and decision-making skills, you become more capable of leading and influencing others. This can make you a more attractive candidate for leadership roles in the future.

Overall, personal development is an excellent way to enhance your career prospects. By acquiring new skills and knowledge, becoming more self-aware, developing greater adaptability, and building leadership skills, you can increase your value to your current employer and become a more competitive candidate in the job market.

Resilience

Resilience is the ability to adapt and cope with adversity and challenges in life. While some people may seem to have an innate resilience, it is also a skill that can be developed and enhanced through personal development. In this chapter, I will explore how personal development can enhance your resilience in several ways.

Firstly, personal development helps you become more self-aware by encouraging you to reflect on your thoughts, feelings, and behaviours. By being aware of your reactions and behaviours, you can identify your strengths and weaknesses, allowing you to better cope with challenges and bounce back from setbacks. With greater self-awareness, you can identify triggers that may cause you to feel overwhelmed and develop strategies to manage them.

Secondly, personal development can help you adopt a growth mindset, which is the belief that your abilities and intelligence can be developed through hard work and dedication. This mindset can help you approach challenges as opportunities for growth and learning, rather than as threats to your self-esteem. When you have a growth mindset, you are more likely to view setbacks as temporary and believe that you can overcome them with effort and determination.

Thirdly, personal development can help you develop emotional regulation skills, which are essential for resilience. These skills allow you to manage your emotions in a healthy way, rather than being overwhelmed by them. By learning how to regulate your emotions, you can stay calm and focused in the face of adversity. You can learn techniques such as mindfulness, meditation, or deep breathing, which can help you stay grounded and centred during stressful situations.

Fourthly, personal development can help you develop a range of coping strategies, such as seeking social support, exercise, or engaging in hobbies. These strategies can help you cope with stress and adversity, and bounce back from setbacks more quickly. By having a variety of coping strategies, you can find the ones that work best for you and use them in different situations.

Lastly, personal development can help you prioritise self-care, such as getting enough sleep, eating a healthy diet, and exercising regularly. When you take care of your physical and mental health, you are better equipped to deal with stress and adversity. By making self-care a priority, you can prevent burnout and maintain your resilience over the long term.

Personal development can help you build the skills and habits necessary for resilience. By becoming more self-aware, adopting a growth mindset, developing emotional regulation skills, and practicing coping strategies and self-care, you can navigate life's challenges with greater ease and confidence. Personal development can help you to develop the resilience you need to face whatever life throws your way.

Fulfilment

Personal development can be an incredibly rewarding journey that can lead to greater fulfilment in your life. By focusing on your personal growth, you can develop a deeper understanding of who you are and what matters most to you. Here are some ways that personal development can increase your sense of fulfilment:

Firstly, personal development can help you clarify your values. Your values are the guiding principles that dictate how you behave and make decisions. When you are clear about your values, you can make choices that align with them, leading to a greater sense of purpose and meaning in your life. By taking the time to reflect on what matters most to you, you can develop a better understanding of yourself and what you want to achieve.

Secondly, personal development can help you set meaningful goals. When you set goals that are aligned with your values, you are more likely to feel motivated and fulfilled when you achieve them. Pursuing these goals can give you a sense of accomplishment and satisfaction, leading to greater fulfilment.

Thirdly, personal development can help you build confidence in your abilities. As you develop new skills and achieve your goals, you will feel more capable and empowered. This sense of self-efficacy can lead to greater fulfilment and a sense of purpose in your life.

Fourthly, personal development can help you improve your relationships with others. Building healthy relationships with friends, family, and colleagues can enhance your sense of connection and belonging. By developing skills like empathy, communication, and conflict resolution, you will be better equipped to build and maintain healthy relationships, leading to greater fulfilment in your life.

Lastly, personal development can help you cultivate gratitude. Practicing gratitude involves focusing on what you have rather than what you lack. By appreciating the good things in your life, you can experience greater happiness and fulfilment. This can lead to a more positive outlook and a greater sense of contentment with your life.

Overall, personal development can help you create a more fulfilling life. By focusing on your personal growth and investing in yourself, you can develop a deeper understanding of yourself, set meaningful goals, build confidence, improve your relationships, and cultivate gratitude. With these skills and habits, you can create a life that is rich in meaning, purpose, and happiness.

CHAPTER 3: TIME MANAGEMENT

In this chapter, we'll be discussing time management, a crucial skill that can help you achieve your goals and maximise your productivity. Effective time management involves planning, prioritising, and focusing on the most important tasks. Let's take a closer look at each of these components.

Firstly, planning is essential in time management. By setting clear goals, creating to-do lists, and creating schedules, you can stay organised and focused on the tasks you need to complete. Without a plan, it's easy to get side-tracked and lose sight of what needs to be done.

Next, prioritising tasks is crucial in time management. By assessing the urgency and importance of tasks, you can determine which tasks require the most attention and should be completed first. This helps you avoid wasting time on less important tasks and ensures that you make progress towards your goals.

In addition, focus is important in time management. Avoiding distractions and staying focused on the task at hand is key to completing tasks efficiently. This includes avoiding interruptions and staying focused on the task at hand.

Time-saving techniques are also helpful in time management. These can include delegating tasks to others, automating repetitive tasks, and outsourcing tasks that are not essential to your goals. By utilising these techniques, you can save time and focus on the tasks that matter most.

Finally, self-discipline is crucial in effective time management. Holding yourself accountable for meeting deadlines and avoiding procrastination is key to making progress towards your goals. This includes setting deadlines for yourself and committing to meeting them.

By practicing effective time management techniques, you can increase your productivity, reduce stress and anxiety, and achieve your goals more efficiently. So, start planning, prioritising, focusing, and utilising time-saving techniques to manage your time effectively and achieve success!

Styles of Time Management

As someone who has always struggled with managing my time effectively, I've come to realise that there are different time management styles that people use to manage their time effectively. Understanding these styles can help you identify your own style and develop strategies to improve your productivity and achieve your goals.

One common time management style is the hopper style, where people jump from one task to another without completing them. This style can lead to a lack of productivity and a sense of being overwhelmed. To combat this, hoppers can try time-blocking techniques, prioritising tasks based on importance, and using tools such as to-do lists or project management software to stay on track.

The hyperfocus time management style, on the other hand, involves becoming deeply immersed in a single task, with a preference for seeing it through to completion. While this style can lead to increased productivity and high-quality output, it also has its drawbacks, including a lack of flexibility and potentially missed deadlines. Implementing techniques such as setting reminders to switch tasks periodically and tracking time allocation for different tasks can enhance productivity for hyperfocus style users.

The Cliff-hanger time management style involves thriving in high-stress situations and working best when under pressure. However, this style can result in rushed and low-quality work, as well as a tendency to procrastinate until the last minute. Strategies such as tracking time for each task, prioritising tasks to avoid last-minute rushes, and scheduling earlier deadlines for urgent tasks can help individuals who use the Cliff-hanger style improve their productivity and achieve higher-quality results.

For those who use the Big Picture time management style, taking a bird's eye view of tasks and plans is key, with more emphasis on planning and strategising rather than the details. While this style offers advantages such as quick thinking and creative problem solving, it can also lead to lower-quality work due to a potential inability to pay attention to smaller tasks and details. To increase productivity, individuals who use the Big Picture style can benefit from collaborating with detail-oriented individuals, communicating clearly and precisely about their goals and objectives, and writing down their daily routine.

The Perfectionist time management style involves paying great attention to detail, leading to the advantage of producing very high-quality work. However, this style often results in missed deadlines due to the endless pursuit of perfection. Strategies such as auditing time to avoid getting caught up in meaningless details, taking on fewer projects at a time, and delegating lower-priority tasks can help Perfectionist style time managers strike a balance between attention to detail and meeting deadlines.

Finally, the Impulsive time management style involves working without a plan and enjoying the spontaneity of the moment. While this style can lead to great improvisation skills, individuals who use this style may struggle to meet deadlines and sustain consistent long-term effort. Incorporating routines, creating schedules, and considering larger projects and objectives before making a decision can help individuals with an Impulsive time management style increase their productivity and achieve greater success.

Regardless of your time management style, prioritisation is a crucial aspect of effective time management. By organising tasks in order of their importance and urgency, you can maximise your productivity and achieve your goals efficiently. Understanding your time management style and implementing strategies to improve your productivity can help you succeed in both your personal and professional life.

Prioritisation

I know how challenging it can be to prioritise tasks effectively. However, by considering a few key factors, you can make the process much easier and more manageable.

The first factor to consider is importance. You need to identify the tasks that are most critical to your goals and prioritise them accordingly. This may involve taking a step back and considering what you want to achieve in the short-term and long-term, and what tasks will help you get there.

Next, you need to determine which tasks require immediate attention and cannot be delayed. This is where urgency comes into play. It's important to recognise which tasks need to be done right away and which ones can wait. This can help you avoid wasting time on less critical tasks and ensure that you're focusing on what's most important.

Another factor to consider is the time required to complete each task. By estimating how long each task will take, you can better plan your schedule and avoid overcommitting yourself. This will help you manage your time more effectively and ensure that you're able to complete tasks within the allotted time frame.

It's also important to assess the resources required for each task, including people, equipment, and materials. This can help you plan ahead and ensure that you have everything you need to complete each task on time and to a high standard.

Finally, you need to consider the consequences of not completing each task on time. This may include missed deadlines, lost opportunities, or other negative outcomes. By understanding the potential consequences, you can better prioritise tasks and ensure that you're focusing on what's most important.

By considering these factors and prioritising tasks accordingly, you can better manage your time and ensure that you're focusing on the most critical tasks at hand. With practice, you'll become more efficient and effective in managing your time, which will help you achieve your goals and succeed in your personal and professional life.

Motivation and Productivity

We all know that without motivation, it can be challenging to remain focused and complete tasks efficiently. But the good news is that there are several ways to increase motivation in time management.

First and foremost, setting clear goals and objectives is essential. When you have a clear understanding of what needs to be accomplished, it can provide a sense of purpose and direction, motivating you to work towards achieving those goals. So take some time to identify your goals and objectives for the day or week ahead and make sure they are realistic and achievable.

Another way to boost motivation is to establish a routine and stick to it. When you have a routine, it can help create a sense of structure and discipline in your workday, providing a framework for productivity. Try to schedule your tasks at the same time each day, and you'll find that you become more efficient in completing them.

It's also essential to take breaks and allow yourself time for rest and relaxation. A rested mind is more productive and motivated than an exhausted one. Incorporating small rewards into your routine can also be motivating, such as taking a short walk or having a favourite snack after completing a task. This can help you recharge and refocus, ready to tackle the next task on your list.

Finally, surrounding yourself with positivity and support can also boost motivation. Working with a team that is encouraging and supportive can help keep you motivated, and seeking out positive affirmations and inspiration can help keep you focused on your goals. Don't be afraid to reach out to others for help and support when needed.

In a nutshell, motivation is a crucial factor in productivity when it comes to time management. By setting clear goals, establishing a routine, taking breaks and incorporating small rewards, and surrounding yourself with positivity and support, you can increase your motivation and achieve greater success in managing your time effectively. So, let's stay motivated and keep pushing forward towards our goals!

CHAPTER 4: HABITS

Have you ever wondered why you tend to do certain things automatically, without really thinking about it? Well, that's because your brain has formed a neural pathway that makes that behaviour automatic and habitual.

The process of habituation involves a feedback loop between the brain's basal ganglia and prefrontal cortex. When we repeatedly perform a behaviour in a specific context or environment, our brains begin to associate that behaviour with that particular context or environment. This association creates a neural pathway in the basal ganglia, which is responsible for our automatic, habitual behaviours.

Initially, when we start performing a new behaviour, our prefrontal cortex is heavily involved in decision-making and planning the behaviour. However, as we repeat the behaviour over time, the prefrontal cortex becomes less active, and the basal ganglia takes over the responsibility for the behaviour, making it more automatic and habitual.

Reinforcement also plays a crucial role in habit formation. When we receive a reward or positive outcome from a behaviour, our brains are more likely to repeat that behaviour in the future. This positive reinforcement strengthens the neural pathway in the basal ganglia, making the behaviour more automatic and habitual.

To put it briefly, habits are formed through a process of repetition and reinforcement, which creates neural pathways in the basal ganglia that make the behaviour automatic and habitual.

Understanding this process can help us develop good habits by repeating positive behaviours and reinforcing them with positive outcomes.

Routines Vs Habits

Let's talk about routines and habits. While they share some similarities, they also have distinct differences that set them apart.

Firstly, routines are established for a particular purpose, such as getting ready for work or school. They are typically consciously planned and executed, and often have a specific outcome in mind. In contrast, habits are often formed without a specific purpose and tend to be automatic and unconscious.

Another difference between the two is their level of flexibility. Routines are usually more rigid and structured, whereas habits are more flexible and adaptable. For example, a morning routine may involve a specific order of tasks, while a habit of exercising can be done at various times throughout the day or week.

Routines also tend to be shorter-term and can change with different life stages. In contrast, habits are often long-term and can be challenging to break once established. For example, a routine of packing lunch for work can easily change once the job or schedule changes, while a habit of procrastination may persist across different situations and environments.

Finally, routines may or may not have a specific outcome in mind, while habits often do. A habit of healthy eating, for example, may have the specific outcome of maintaining good health, while a routine of morning coffee may not have a specific outcome in mind.

In summary, routines are consciously planned and structured behaviours that are established for a specific purpose, while habits are automatic, long-term behaviours that often have a specific outcome in mind.

Set your Intentions.

Setting intentions is an empowering practice that allows us to take control of our lives and create a clear path towards success. When we set intentions, we are essentially directing our thoughts, emotions, and actions towards achieving specific goals or aspirations.

To begin setting intentions, take some time to reflect on what you truly want to accomplish or experience in your life. Think about your personal or professional goals, your relationships, your health, or any other area of your life that you want to improve. Be honest with yourself and identify what truly matters to you.

Once you have identified your intentions, write them down and visualise yourself achieving them. Focus on the positive emotions and feelings that you will experience when you accomplish your intentions and use this as motivation to take action towards achieving them. Remember, the more you can visualise and feel the accomplishment of your intentions, the more likely you are to achieve them.

It's also important to take action towards your intentions by breaking them down into smaller, achievable steps. Create a plan for how you will work towards your intentions, and take consistent action towards them every day. By taking small steps towards your intentions every day, you'll build momentum and make progress towards achieving your goals.

Setting intentions is not a one-time event, but an ongoing process that requires commitment and dedication. You may need to adjust your intentions as circumstances change, or you may encounter obstacles along the way. However, by remaining focused on your intentions and taking consistent action towards them, you can create the life that you desire and achieve your goals. So, take some time to set your intentions and start working towards the life that you want to create!

Roadblocks

Preparing for roadblocks is an essential part of achieving any goal or intention. No matter how carefully you plan, unexpected setbacks or difficult situations can arise that can derail your progress. That's why it's important to be proactive and prepare for roadblocks before they happen.

The first step in preparing for roadblocks is to identify potential obstacles or challenges that may arise. This requires some introspection and reflection on your goals and the path you are taking towards achieving them. Once you have identified potential roadblocks, write them down and brainstorm possible solutions for overcoming them.

Creating a contingency plan is the next step in preparing for roadblocks. This plan should outline specific strategies and actions you can take to deal with potential obstacles. It may involve having alternative approaches or solutions in place, seeking support from others, or simply being flexible and adaptable in your approach.

Staying motivated is also crucial when facing roadblocks. It's easy to get discouraged when things don't go as planned, but it's important to remember why you started and keep your vision of success in mind. Stay focused on your goals and find ways to re-energise yourself when you feel demotivated.

Practicing resilience is another important aspect of preparing for roadblocks. Resilience is the ability to bounce back from setbacks and challenges. It involves developing a growth mindset, staying optimistic, and viewing roadblocks as opportunities for learning and growth. By practicing resilience, you can develop the inner strength to overcome any challenge that comes your way.

Finally, staying connected is crucial when facing roadblocks. Seek support from friends, family, or a coach or mentor who can help you stay accountable, motivated, and inspired. Surround yourself with positive and supportive people who believe in your goals and can help you stay on track.

In conclusion, preparing for roadblocks is an essential part of achieving any goal or intention. By identifying potential obstacles, creating a contingency plan, staying motivated, practicing resilience, and staying connected, you can overcome any challenge that comes your way and achieve your goals. Remember, success is not a straight line, but a journey with ups and downs. With preparation and perseverance, you can overcome any roadblock and achieve your dreams.

Start Small

Starting with small things and taking one step at a time is a powerful way to create better habits. Habits are the building blocks of our lives, and small changes can make a big difference in our overall well-being and success.

To start creating better habits, the first step is to identify one small habit that you want to create or change. It could be anything from drinking more water to taking a 10-minute walk each day. The key is to make it achievable and realistic so that you can build momentum and gain confidence in your ability to make changes.

Once you have identified your small habit, set a goal for how often you will perform it. This could be every day or a certain number of times per week. Creating a reminder can also be helpful to help you remember to perform the habit. Use a phone alarm, a sticky note, or a visual cue to keep it top of mind.

As you start to perform your small habit, remember to celebrate your progress along the way. Each small success is a step towards creating better habits, and celebrating those successes can help you stay motivated and build momentum.

Finally, once you have established your small habit, gradually increase it over time. This could mean adding more repetitions or increasing the duration of the habit. The key is to keep building on your success and continue to challenge yourself.

Remember, creating better habits is a journey, not a destination. By starting with small things and taking one step at a time, you can build momentum and make lasting changes to your habits over time. So, start small, be patient, and enjoy the journey!

CHAPTER 5:
PRODUCTIVITY

When we talk about productivity, we often think of it as a measure of how much work we get done. However, it's important to remember that productivity is not just about getting things done, but about getting the right things done in the most efficient and effective way possible.

To improve your productivity, it's essential to prioritise your tasks and manage your time effectively. This means identifying the most important tasks and focusing on them first, instead of getting bogged down in small, less important tasks that can take up a lot of time. It also means avoiding distractions and staying focused on your goals and objectives.

One of the biggest factors that can impact productivity is procrastination. We all have moments when we don't feel like doing something, but it's important to push through these feelings and get started on the task at hand. Procrastination can also be caused by lack of motivation, so it's important to stay motivated and focused on your goals.

Another key factor that can impact productivity is the use of tools and techniques to streamline workflows and increase efficiency. This could include using apps and software to automate repetitive tasks, or developing systems and processes to make work more efficient and effective.

Ultimately, productivity is about achieving your goals and making the most of your time and resources. By focusing on the most important tasks, managing your time effectively, and using tools and techniques to increase efficiency, you can increase your productivity and achieve success in all areas of your life. So, start focusing on your priorities, stay motivated, and work smarter, not just harder, to achieve your goals.

Productivity Styles

When it comes to productivity, there is no one-size-fits-all approach. Each person has their own unique style that works best for them, and it's important to understand your own style in order to maximise your productivity.

One common productivity style is the Planner. If you're a planner, you like to have a structured plan for your day, and you may create detailed to-do lists or schedules. You prefer to work from a set plan and can become anxious if there are unexpected changes or disruptions.

The Prioritiser, on the other hand, focuses on identifying the most important tasks and working on those first. They are skilled at setting priorities and are often able to complete their most important work early in the day.

The Multi-Tasker enjoys juggling multiple tasks at once and can switch between different projects or activities quickly. However, this approach can sometimes lead to decreased focus and quality of work.

The Time-Blocker sets aside specific blocks of time for different tasks or projects. This approach can be helpful for staying focused and preventing distractions.

The Procrastinator tends to put off tasks until the last minute and may thrive under the pressure of a tight deadline. However, this approach can be stressful and can lead to lower quality work.

Finally, the Collaborator prefers to work in groups or with a partner and may find that they are more productive when bouncing ideas off of others. This approach can be helpful for brainstorming and problem-solving.

It's important to note that these productivity styles are not mutually exclusive, and many people may use a combination of different styles depending on the task or project at hand. For example, you may be a planner for your work tasks, but a collaborator when it comes to personal projects or hobbies.

The key is to find what works best for you and to use that approach to increase your productivity and achieve your goals. Don't be afraid to experiment with different styles and techniques until you find the one that works best for you.

Techniques to help.

First and foremost, it's important to set goals and prioritise tasks. Identify the most important tasks or projects and work on those first. Break down larger goals into smaller, more manageable tasks. This can help you stay focused and motivated as you work towards your objectives.

Next, consider using a planner or to-do list to keep track of tasks and deadlines. This can help you stay organised and focused on what needs to be done. It's important to review your planner or to-do list regularly to ensure you are staying on track and completing tasks in a timely manner.

One of the biggest productivity killers is distractions. To minimise distractions, try eliminating or minimising potential distractions such as social media notifications or email alerts when working on important tasks. Consider using tools like website blockers or noise-cancelling headphones to help you stay focused.

Taking regular breaks throughout the day is also important to recharge and prevent burnout. Consider using the Pomodoro technique, which involves working for a set amount of time (typically 25 minutes) and then taking a short break. This can help you stay focused and energised throughout the day.

If possible, delegate tasks to others or outsource them to free up time for more important work. This can help you stay focused on the tasks that are most important and require your expertise.

It's also important to practice self-care. Take care of your physical and mental health by getting enough sleep, exercise, and proper nutrition. This can help improve your energy levels and focus.

Lastly, learn to say no. Prioritise your time and avoid taking on unnecessary tasks or commitments. Learn to say no when your plate is already full. This can help you stay focused on the tasks that are most important and require your attention.

Remember, productivity is about working smarter, not harder. By implementing these simple productivity strategies, you can increase your efficiency and effectiveness, achieve your goals, and improve your overall well-being.

CHAPTER 6: GOALS

Goals give us something to work towards, and they can help us to stay focused and motivated even when we encounter obstacles or setbacks along the way. Without goals, we might find ourselves wandering aimlessly, unsure of what we want to achieve or how to get there.

It's important to note that not all goals are created equal. To be effective, goals should be specific, measurable, and achievable. This means taking the time to identify exactly what you want to achieve and setting clear parameters for success. For example, instead of setting a goal to "get in shape," you might set a specific goal to "run a 5k in under 30 minutes within the next six months."

Measurable goals allow you to track your progress and determine when you have achieved them. For example, if your goal is to save £5,000 for a down payment on a house, you can track your progress by setting incremental milestones along the way.

Finally, achievable goals are realistic and within your abilities and resources to attain. While it's important to challenge yourself, setting unrealistic goals can lead to frustration and disappointment. Instead, set goals that push you outside of your comfort zone, but that are still within reach.

By setting specific, measurable, and achievable goals, you can stay focused and motivated, measure progress and track accomplishments, and ultimately achieve success in all areas of your life. Whether you're setting goals for your career, education, health, or personal development, taking the time to identify and work towards your objectives is a powerful tool for personal and professional growth.

The S.M.A.S.H. I.T Method

As human beings, we are wired to set goals and work towards achieving them. Whether it's personal or professional, goal setting is an integral part of our lives. However, setting goals can be a daunting task, especially if we don't have a clear process in place. That's where the SMASH IT method comes in.

SMASH IT is a simple yet effective goal-setting process that can help you achieve your goals with ease. The acronym stands for Specific, Make a Deadline, Analyse the Goal, Sort and Prioritise Tasks, Have a Deadline for Each Task, Imagine and Visualise, and Take Action.

S

The first step in the SMASH IT process, which is a framework for goal setting, is to Set a Specific Goal. This step is crucial because it sets the foundation for the rest of the process.

When setting a specific goal, it's important to choose a goal that is clear and well-defined. This means that the goal should be specific, measurable, and achievable. A specific goal provides clarity about what you want to achieve, and helps you stay focused and motivated throughout the process.

Measurable goals allow you to track your progress and know when you've achieved your goal. It's important to be able to quantify your progress, whether it's by tracking your weight loss, number of sales, or the number of new skills you've learned.

Achievable goals are realistic and attainable. It's important to set goals that challenge you, but that are also within your reach. Setting unattainable goals can lead to frustration and disappointment, while setting achievable goals can boost your confidence and help you stay motivated.

When setting a specific goal, it's important to also consider why it's important to you. This can provide the necessary motivation and inspiration to stay committed to achieving your goal. Understanding your "why" can help you stay on track when things get tough and can remind you of the bigger picture.

I hope you can see that setting a specific goal is the first step in the SMASH IT process, and it's essential for success in achieving your goals. By choosing a goal that is specific, measurable, achievable, and meaningful to you, you can stay focused and motivated throughout the process, and ultimately achieve the results you desire.

M

The second step in the SMASH IT process is to Make a Deadline. Setting a realistic deadline for achieving your goal is critical to maintaining your motivation and focus throughout the goal-setting process. Without a deadline, it's easy to lose sight of your goal and become distracted by other priorities or activities.

When setting a deadline, it's important to choose a timeframe that is both realistic and challenging. If the deadline is too far away, you may be less motivated to take action, and if it's too close, you may become overwhelmed and discouraged. A realistic deadline takes into account any obstacles or challenges you may face along the way, as well as your current level of skill, experience, and available resources.

A deadline also helps to create a sense of urgency and accountability, which can be powerful motivators. With a deadline in place, you have a clear target to work towards, and you are more likely to take consistent action towards achieving your goal.

Additionally, setting a deadline helps you to prioritise your actions and stay focused on the most important tasks. When you have a clear timeframe in mind, you can more easily identify the key milestones and steps required to achieve your goal, and work towards them systematically.

Making a deadline is an essential step in the SMASH IT process. By setting a realistic and challenging deadline for achieving your goal, you can stay motivated, focused, and accountable throughout the process. A deadline helps to create urgency, prioritise actions, and achieve success in a timely manner.

A

The third step in the SMASH IT process is to Analyse the Goal. This step involves breaking down your goal into smaller, more manageable tasks. This process allows you to identify the specific steps you need to take in order to achieve your goal and helps you to stay focused and motivated throughout the process.

When analysing your goal, it's important to consider any obstacles or challenges you may face along the way. By identifying potential roadblocks in advance, you can develop strategies to overcome them, and stay on track towards achieving your goal.

In addition, it's important to assess your current level of skill, knowledge, and resources. By identifying any gaps in your abilities, you can develop a plan to acquire the skills or knowledge you need to achieve your goal. This may involve taking courses, seeking mentorship or advice, or collaborating with others who have complementary skills.

Another important aspect of goal analysis is identifying the resources and support you may need along the way. This could include financial resources, time, or support from friends, family, or colleagues. By identifying these needs in advance, you can develop a plan to acquire the necessary resources and support and ensure that you have the tools you need to achieve your goal.

By breaking your goal down into smaller, more manageable tasks, and considering the obstacles, skills, and resources required to achieve it, you can develop a roadmap to success. This analysis helps to ensure that you stay focused and motivated throughout the process, and that you are able to overcome any challenges that arise along the way.

S

The fourth step in the SMASH IT process is to Sort and Prioritise Tasks. This step involves ordering and prioritising the tasks required to achieve your goal. By sorting your tasks in this way, you can ensure that you stay organised, focused, and on track throughout the process.

To sort and prioritise your tasks, start by listing all of the tasks that you have identified during the goal analysis phase. Once you have your list, consider the importance and urgency of each task.

Tasks that are both important and urgent should be given top priority. These are the tasks that require immediate attention and cannot be put off. For example, if your goal is to write a book, then finishing a chapter by a certain deadline might be an important and urgent task.

Next, consider tasks that are important but not urgent. These are tasks that have a significant impact on your overall goal but may not require immediate attention. These tasks should be prioritised after urgent tasks.

Finally, consider tasks that are urgent but not important. These tasks may be time-sensitive, but they don't necessarily have a significant impact on achieving your overall goal. These tasks should be prioritised after important tasks.

By sorting and prioritising your tasks in this way, you can ensure that you are focused on the most critical tasks at any given time. This helps to ensure that you are making progress towards your goal in the most efficient and effective way possible.

H

The fifth step in the SMASH IT process is to Have a Deadline for Each Task. Once you have sorted and prioritised your tasks, it's important to assign a deadline to each task to keep yourself on track and motivated.

Assigning a deadline to each task helps you to stay accountable and ensures that you are making progress towards your goal. When setting deadlines, it's important to be realistic and consider the amount of time required to complete each task. If you set unrealistic deadlines, you may become discouraged and lose motivation.

To set effective deadlines, consider the urgency and importance of each task. Tasks that are both urgent and important should be given earlier deadlines, while less urgent or important tasks can be given later deadlines.

It's also important to be flexible with your deadlines. Life can be unpredictable, and unexpected circumstances may arise that could cause you to miss a deadline. If this happens, don't be too hard on yourself. Instead, re-evaluate your plan and adjust your deadlines as necessary.

By setting deadlines for each task, you can ensure that you are making steady progress towards your goal. This helps you to stay motivated and accountable, and ensures that you are more likely to achieve success in the end.

I

The sixth step in the SMASH IT process is to Imagine and Visualise. Visualisation is a powerful technique that can help you to stay motivated and focused on achieving your goal. By visualising yourself achieving your goal and completing each task, you can stay connected to your goal and maintain a positive mindset throughout the process.

Visualisation involves creating mental images of yourself

achieving your goal. When you visualise, you imagine the outcome of your efforts in vivid detail. You might imagine how you will feel once you have achieved your goal, what you will look like, and what you will be doing. You can also visualise yourself completing each task required to achieve your goal. Visualising yourself overcoming obstacles and challenges along the way can also help you to stay motivated and focused.

When you visualise, you activate the same parts of your brain that would be active if you were actually performing the task. This can help to reinforce the neural pathways that are involved in goal achievement, making it easier for you to stay on track and achieve success.

To practice visualisation, find a quiet place where you can relax and focus on your goal. Close your eyes and imagine yourself achieving your goal in vivid detail. Imagine yourself completing each task required to achieve your goal, and see yourself overcoming any obstacles or challenges along the way. You can also imagine how you will feel once you have achieved your goal and the positive impact it will have on your life.

Visualisation is a powerful tool that can help you to stay motivated and focused on achieving your goal. By practicing visualisation regularly, you can stay connected to your goal and maintain a positive mindset throughout the process.

T

The final step in the SMASH IT framework is to take action. While it's essential to set specific goals, create deadlines, analyse the goal, sort and prioritise tasks, assign deadlines to each task, and visualise yourself achieving your goal, none of these steps matter if you don't take action.

Taking action means putting in the effort and energy to complete each task and work towards achieving your goal. It requires dedication, commitment, and discipline to follow through on the plan you have created for yourself.

It's important to remember that success is not achieved overnight, but through consistent and persistent action. By taking action towards your goal every day, even if it's just a small step, you are making progress and moving closer to achieving your desired outcome.

Taking action can be challenging, especially when faced with obstacles or setbacks. It's crucial to stay motivated and focused on your end goal, reminding yourself why it's essential to you and the impact it will have on your life.

To put it simply, the SMASH IT method is a simple and effective goal-setting process that can help you achieve your goals with ease. By following the SMASH IT acronym, you can break down your goals into smaller, more manageable tasks and take concrete steps towards achieving them. So, go ahead, SMASH IT, and achieve your goals!

CHAPTER 7:
PROCRASTINATION

Procrastination - the word itself can trigger a wave of guilt and anxiety for many of us. We know we have work to do, but we put it off until the last minute. It can be frustrating to feel like we're not making progress towards our goals, but we keep doing it anyway. But why do we procrastinate, and what can we do about it?

Procrastination is often the result of a complex set of factors. For some, it may be fear of failure or fear of success that holds them back. Others may struggle with perfectionism or find themselves overwhelmed by the task at hand. Regardless of the root cause, procrastination can lead to negative consequences, such as missed deadlines, lower quality work, and increased stress.

The good news is that overcoming procrastination is possible. One of the first steps is to identify why you're procrastinating in the first place. Once you understand the underlying reasons, you can begin to develop strategies to address them.

Breaking tasks down into smaller, more manageable steps can be an effective way to overcome procrastination. Instead of focusing on the overwhelming task as a whole, you can tackle it one small piece at a time. Creating a schedule or plan can also help you stay on track and prioritise your work.

Distractions are a common culprit in procrastination. It's easy to get side-tracked by social media, email, or other tempting activities. One way to minimise distractions is to create a designated work area that is free from any potential distractions.

You can also consider using productivity tools, such as website blockers or noise-cancelling headphones, to help you stay focused.

Developing good habits and cultivating a positive mindset can also help you overcome procrastination. By rewarding yourself for progress towards your goals, you can create positive feedback loops that reinforce good habits. Additionally, focusing on the benefits of completing a task rather than the effort required can help shift your mindset from one of avoidance to one of motivation.

As you can see, procrastination is a common challenge that many of us face, but it is not insurmountable. By understanding the root causes of our behaviour and developing strategies to address them, we can overcome procrastination and achieve our goals. Remember, it's not about being perfect, but about making progress towards our aspirations.

Triggers

Procrastination can be a frustrating and self-defeating habit that can interfere with productivity, work quality, and goal attainment. While we may often blame our lack of willpower or discipline for procrastination, it's important to understand that there are specific triggers that cause us to delay or avoid tasks that need to be done.

One common trigger of procrastination is a lack of motivation or enthusiasm about a task. When we don't feel excited or interested in what we're doing, it can be easy to put it off and find something else to do. Similarly, fear of failure can cause us to avoid tasks that we think might be difficult or risky, while perfectionism can lead us to delay starting or completing tasks because we fear they won't be perfect or up to our standards.

Feeling overwhelmed by the size or complexity of a task or project can also trigger procrastination. When we don't know where to start or how to move forward, it can be challenging to take action.

Additionally, if we lack effective time management skills or tools, it can be hard to prioritise tasks and manage our time effectively, which can lead to procrastination.

Sometimes, we may also procrastinate simply because we lack clarity or direction. When we're unsure about what we need to do or how to do it, it can be hard to get started. Finally, distractions such as social media, TV, or other people can be a significant trigger for procrastination. When we're surrounded by distractions, it can be difficult to stay focused and on task.

By identifying our personal triggers for procrastination, we can take steps to address them and develop strategies to stay on track and overcome procrastination. For example, if lack of motivation is a trigger, we can try to find ways to make the task more interesting or rewarding. If we struggle with fear of failure, we can remind ourselves that making mistakes is a natural part of the learning process. By addressing our triggers and developing strategies to manage them, we can increase our productivity, reduce stress, and achieve our goals more effectively.

What does it Cost?

Have you ever put off a task until the last minute or avoided it altogether? Maybe you've experienced the temporary relief of not having to face a challenging or unpleasant task, only to realise later that procrastination has cost you in some way. Procrastination is a common behaviour that can have serious consequences, both in our personal and professional lives.

One of the biggest costs of procrastination is missed opportunities. When we delay or avoid taking action on important tasks or goals, we may miss out on opportunities to advance our careers, improve our relationships, or achieve our desired outcomes. For example, if you delay applying for a job or pitching a new idea to your boss, someone else may seize the opportunity before you.

Procrastination can also lead to increased stress and anxiety. When we put off tasks, we may worry about the consequences of not completing them or meeting our deadlines. This stress and anxiety can be especially detrimental to our mental and physical health over time.

In addition, procrastination can reduce our overall productivity. When we waste time on unimportant tasks or distractions, we have less time and energy to devote to important tasks. This can make it harder to accomplish our goals and can leave us feeling unfulfilled and frustrated.

When we rush to complete tasks at the last minute, we may produce lower quality work, which can damage our reputation, relationships, or opportunities for advancement. And finally, procrastination can damage our self-esteem and confidence, leading to feelings of guilt, shame, and inadequacy.

By recognising the costs of procrastination, we can take steps to overcome it and achieve our goals more effectively. With the right strategies and mindset, we can break the cycle of procrastination and unlock our full potential.

How to stop Procrastinating

Stopping procrastination can be a challenging task, but it is possible with some effort and dedication. Here are some steps that you can follow to help you overcome procrastination:

1. Identify the reasons for your procrastination: Understanding why you procrastinate is key to overcoming it. Take some time to reflect and identify the underlying reasons that make you put things off. Is it fear of failure, lack of motivation, or overwhelm? Once you know the reasons, you can work on addressing them.

2. Break tasks into smaller steps: Large tasks can seem overwhelming, making it harder to get started. Breaking

them down into smaller, manageable steps can help you take action and build momentum. Start with the smallest and easiest task and then move on to more challenging ones.

3. Set achievable goals and deadlines: Setting specific, achievable goals and deadlines can help you stay focused and motivated. This can help you make progress and avoid the urge to procrastinate. Make sure your goals are realistic and attainable.

4. Eliminate distractions: Minimising distractions, such as social media or TV, can help you stay focused on your tasks. Create a work environment that is conducive to productivity, with minimal distractions. Turn off notifications on your phone and log out of social media accounts.

5. Use positive self-talk: Negative self-talk can increase anxiety and reduce motivation, making it easier to procrastinate. Use positive self-talk to build confidence and motivation. Remind yourself of your strengths, accomplishments, and capabilities.

6. Reward yourself for progress: Celebrate small successes along the way to keep yourself motivated and on track. Give yourself a small reward for each step taken, such as a break or a treat. This can help you stay motivated and make the process more enjoyable.

7. Seek support: Get support from others, such as a friend or a coach, to help you stay accountable and on track. They can provide encouragement and motivation when you need it most. Share your goals with someone you trust and ask them to check in with you periodically.

By implementing these strategies, you can overcome procrastination and achieve your goals more effectively. Remember that breaking the habit of procrastination takes time and effort, but it is worth it in the end. Start small, be consistent, and don't give up. You got this!

CHAPTER 8: STRESS

Stress is something that we all experience at some point in our lives. It's a natural response to challenging or threatening situations, and can help us perform better under pressure. However, excessive or chronic stress can have negative effects on our mental and physical health.

When we encounter a stressful situation, the body releases hormones like adrenaline and cortisol, which prepare us for a "fight or flight" response. This can be helpful in short bursts, but when stress becomes chronic, it can lead to a range of health problems.

Stress can be caused by a variety of factors, such as work pressure, financial difficulties, relationship issues, health problems, and major life changes. It's important to recognise the sources of stress in our lives and take steps to manage it effectively.

Managing Stress

Some strategies that can help manage stress include exercise, meditation, deep breathing, spending time in nature, getting enough sleep, and practicing self-care. It's also important to prioritise tasks, set realistic goals, and ask for help when needed.

By implementing these strategies and taking steps to manage stress, we can improve our overall well-being and lead happier, healthier lives. Remember, stress is a normal part of life, but it doesn't have to control us. With the right tools and resources, we can overcome it and thrive.

Stress is a natural part of life, but when it becomes too much to handle, it can have negative effects on our physical and mental well-being. That's why it's important to learn how to manage stress. Here are some tips that can help.

The first step is to identify the source of your stress. This can be a difficult task, but it's important to take the time to figure out what's causing your stress. Once you know the source, you can find ways to manage it.

One effective way to manage stress is through exercise. Physical activity releases endorphins, which are natural mood-boosters. It also helps you sleep better at night, which can reduce stress levels.

Relaxation techniques, such as meditation, deep breathing, and yoga, can also be helpful in managing stress. These techniques can help slow your heart rate, calm your mind, and relax your muscles.

Getting enough sleep is also crucial in managing stress. Lack of sleep can increase stress levels, so make sure you're getting 7-8 hours of sleep per night.

Eating a healthy diet is another important way to manage stress. Eating plenty of fruits, vegetables, whole grains, and lean protein can help keep your body healthy and reduce stress levels.

Taking breaks is also crucial in managing stress. When you're feeling overwhelmed, take a break and do something you enjoy. Whether it's going for a walk, reading a book, or watching your favourite TV show, taking time for yourself can help you recharge.

Finally, don't be afraid to talk to someone about your stress. Sometimes, just talking to someone can help you feel better. Whether it's a friend, family member, or a mental health professional, reaching out for support can be a valuable tool in managing stress.

Remember, managing stress is a process, and what works for one person may not work for another. Experiment with different techniques and find what works best for you. With time and effort, you can learn to manage stress and live a happier, healthier life.

CHAPTER 9:
COMMUNICATION

Communication is a fundamental part of our everyday lives. It allows us to connect with others and share our thoughts, ideas, and emotions. Communication can take many forms, from a simple nod of the head to a lengthy conversation, and it is an essential component of building relationships and achieving our goals.

Verbal communication involves using words to convey a message, and it is the most common form of communication. It can take place face-to-face or through phone calls, video chats, or text messages. Nonverbal communication, on the other hand, involves using body language, facial expressions, and gestures to convey a message. It can add depth and meaning to verbal communication and is especially important when language barriers exist.

Effective communication requires both the sender and receiver to have a shared understanding of the message being conveyed. This means that the message needs to be clear, concise, and delivered in a way that the receiver can easily understand. Active listening is also crucial in effective communication, where the receiver not only hears the message but also pays attention to nonverbal cues and seeks clarification when needed.

Communication is essential for building relationships, resolving conflicts, and achieving our goals. It plays a vital role in our personal and professional lives, and its importance cannot be overstated. With advancements in technology, communication has become even more critical, as it allows us to connect with people from different cultures and backgrounds, promoting global interaction and understanding.

Effective communication is essential for our well-being and success. It involves both verbal and nonverbal communication, and it requires active listening and a shared understanding of the message being conveyed. Whether we are communicating with our loved ones, colleagues, or people from different parts of the world, communication is a powerful tool that can help us connect and achieve our goals.

Why should I Improve my Communication?

Communication is a vital aspect of our lives, and improving our communication skills can bring numerous benefits in both our personal and professional lives. The ability to effectively convey our thoughts, ideas, and feelings is essential for building healthy relationships and achieving our goals.

One of the most significant benefits of improving our communication skills is building better relationships. Communication is the foundation of any healthy relationship, and by improving our ability to connect with others, we can develop deeper relationships, build trust, and foster understanding.

Effective communication also leads to increased productivity. When we can communicate our ideas and expectations clearly, we can work more efficiently, reduce misunderstandings, and achieve our goals more effectively. By communicating effectively with our colleagues and peers, we can also collaborate more effectively, leading to better results and outcomes.

Good communication skills can also enhance problem-solving. When we can communicate our thoughts and ideas effectively, we can identify issues and find solutions more quickly and efficiently. By working collaboratively with others, we can pool our skills and resources to address problems and find the best possible solutions.

Improving our communication skills can also lead to career advancement. Employers highly value good communication skills, and by developing these skills, we can increase our chances of getting hired, receiving promotions, and achieving success in our careers.

Reducing stress is another significant benefit of improving our communication skills. Misunderstandings and conflicts can lead to stress and tension in our relationships and work environments. By communicating effectively and reducing the likelihood of misunderstandings and conflicts, we can lead a more stress-free life.

Finally, enhancing our communication skills can lead to personal growth. When we improve our ability to express our thoughts and emotions, we become more self-aware and gain a greater sense of self-confidence. This, in turn, can help us grow and develop in our personal lives and achieve our goals.

To sum up, improving our communication skills can bring numerous benefits to our lives, including better relationships, increased productivity, improved problem-solving, career advancement, reduced stress, and personal growth. By developing our communication skills, we can achieve our goals, build deeper relationships, and live more fulfilling lives.

Verbal Communication

Verbal communication is an essential part of our everyday lives, and it is important to master the skills necessary to communicate effectively. Whether we are having a conversation with a friend, giving a presentation at work, or interviewing for a job, our ability to communicate clearly and confidently can greatly impact the outcome of the situation.

One of the most critical components of effective verbal communication is clarity. When communicating verbally, it is essential to speak clearly and concisely to ensure that the message is understood. This means avoiding rambling, using filler words, or going off-topic. It is also important to use language that is appropriate for the situation and audience, so as not to cause confusion or offense.

Active listening is another critical aspect of effective verbal communication. It involves paying close attention to the speaker, asking clarifying questions, and providing feedback to show that you understand the message. By being an active listener, you demonstrate respect for the speaker, and you can establish a mutual understanding of the message being conveyed.

Tone and language are also important components of verbal communication. The tone of your voice can convey emotions, attitudes, and intentions, while language choice can influence the meaning and impact of the message. It is essential to use appropriate tone and language for the audience and situation to ensure that the message is received positively.

Nonverbal communication, such as facial expressions, gestures, and body language, also plays a significant role in verbal communication. Nonverbal cues can enhance or detract from the message being conveyed and can influence how the message is received and interpreted. For example, maintaining eye contact can convey confidence and attentiveness, while avoiding eye contact can signal a lack of interest or dishonesty.

Improving your verbal communication skills takes time and practice, but there are many ways to do so. You can start by practicing your delivery, such as by recording yourself and watching for filler words or hesitations. You can also work on active listening by paying attention to others during conversations and meetings. Finally, you can focus on using appropriate tone and language by considering the context and audience of each communication.

So, verbal communication is a critical part of human interaction, and mastering the skills necessary for effective communication can have numerous benefits in both our personal and professional lives. By focusing on clarity, active listening, tone and language, and nonverbal communication, we can become better communicators and establish deeper relationships, achieve our goals, and experience personal growth.

Non-Verbal Communication

Have you ever been in a conversation with someone and noticed that their body language was telling you something different than what they were saying? That's because body language is a powerful tool in communication. It includes nonverbal cues, gestures, and movements that can convey emotions, intentions, and attitudes.

Facial expressions are one of the most important forms of body language. They can communicate a wide range of emotions, from happiness and excitement to sadness and anger. For example, a smile can indicate happiness or friendliness, while a frown can convey displeasure or disapproval. Raising your eyebrows can show surprise, while rolling your eyes can indicate frustration or boredom.

Eye contact is another crucial aspect of body language. It can convey interest, respect, or even attraction. Maintaining eye contact during a conversation shows that you are engaged and attentive. However, prolonged eye contact can be perceived as aggressive or confrontational in some cultures, so it's important to be aware of cultural norms.

Posture is also an important element of body language. Standing up straight with your shoulders back can convey confidence and authority, while slouching or hunching over can indicate insecurity or low self-esteem. Sitting with your legs crossed can be seen as defensive or closed off, while sitting with your arms open can be interpreted as welcoming and friendly.

Hand gestures can also be used to emphasise points or

convey emotions. For example, pointing can be used to draw attention to something, while shrugging can indicate uncertainty or indifference. However, it's important to use hand gestures sparingly and purposefully, as too much movement can be distracting.

It's also important to note that body language can differ depending on cultural and social norms. For example, in some cultures, avoiding eye contact can be a sign of respect, while in others, it can be interpreted as a lack of interest or honesty. It's important to be aware of these differences and adjust your body language accordingly.

By being aware of your own body language and the body language of others, you can become a better communicator. Positive body language cues such as maintaining eye contact, standing up straight, and nodding in agreement can convey confidence and respect. Similarly, observing the body language of others can help you gain insight into their emotions and intentions, which can help you respond appropriately.

As you can see, body language is a powerful tool in communication. By being aware of and using positive body language cues, you can become a better communicator and build stronger relationships with others. So, pay attention to your body language and the body language of those around you, and use it to your advantage!

CHAPTER 10: BRINGING IT ALL TOGETHER.

As I reflect on this book, I can't help but feel a sense of accomplishment. This book has covered the 7 pillars of personal development, which are essential to achieving a fulfilling and successful life. We have talked about the importance of taking care of our mind, body, soul, finances, career, family, and social life. These pillars provide a solid foundation for personal growth and development.

In Chapter 2, we explored the power of personal development and how it can lead to a better understanding of ourselves and improved relationships with others. We learned how personal development can enhance our career prospects, increase our resilience, and ultimately bring more fulfilment into our lives.

Chapter 3 was all about time management. We discussed different styles of time management, prioritisation, motivation, and productivity strategies. By mastering these techniques, we can become more efficient with our time and achieve our goals more effectively.

Chapter 4 focused on developing better habits. We learned how to form new habits by setting intentions, preparing for roadblocks, and starting with small steps. By creating good habits, we can eliminate bad habits and achieve long-lasting personal development.

In Chapter 5, we explored productivity styles and simple strategies to improve efficiency. We discussed the importance of taking breaks, delegating tasks, and using technology to our advantage.

Chapter 6 emphasised the importance of setting and achieving goals. We learned how to create short-term and long-term goals and how to develop a plan to achieve them. By setting goals, we can create a roadmap for our personal development journey.

Chapter 7 was all about overcoming procrastination. We discussed identifying triggers and taking action to stop procrastinating. By eliminating procrastination, we can become more productive and achieve our goals faster.

Chapter 8 focused on stress management. We discussed defining stress and managing it through different techniques such as exercise, meditation, and time management.

Finally, in Chapter 9, we explored the importance of communication and how it can be improved through verbal communication and body language. We learned how to communicate effectively to build better relationships and achieve personal development.

This book has provided a comprehensive understanding of personal development and its various aspects. By applying the principles and strategies discussed throughout, individuals can lead a more fulfilling and successful life. Personal development is an ongoing journey that requires consistent effort and dedication. With the knowledge gained in this book, we can take action towards our growth and development.

So let's go and do it!

www.ingramcontent.com/pod-product-compliance
Lightning Source LLC
Chambersburg PA
CBHW071141220526
45467CB00015B/1693